LET GO

An Hachette UK Company
www.hachette.co.uk

Vie Books, an imprint of Summersdale Pub
Part of Octopus Publishing Group Limited
Carmelite House
50 Victoria Embankment
LONDON
EC4Y 0DZ
UK

www.summersdale.com

Printed and bound in the Czech Republic

ISBN: 978-1-78685-756-9

Substantial discounts on bulk quantities of Summersdale books are available to corporations, professional associations and other organisations. For details contact general enquiries: telephone: +44 (0) 1243 771107 or email: enquiries@summersdale.com.

Disclaimer
Every effort has been made to ensure that the information in this book is accurate and current at the time of publication. The author and the publisher cannot accept responsibility for any misuse or misunderstanding of any information contained herein, or any loss, damage or injury, be it health, financial or otherwise, suffered by any individual or group acting upon or relying on information contained herein. None of the opinions or suggestions in this book is intended to replace medical opinion. If you have concerns about your health, please seek professional advice.

let go

RELEASE YOURSELF FROM ANXIETY

ELIZABETH ARCHER

CONTENTS

Introduction

No matter who you are, the chances are you will have felt anxious at some point in your life. Maybe it was a stressful situation at work or school, an issue with a relationship, or a health condition that was making you feel down. Perhaps the reason you've picked up this book is you're feeling anxious right now. But while anxiety is a part of life, it doesn't need to take over your every thought. Using the tips in this book, you can let go of anxiety and start living the life you want to.

WHAT IS ANXIETY?

Put simply, anxiety is a feeling of worry and unease. Unlike fear, it doesn't pass in a few moments when the immediate threat has been dealt with. Instead it persists – sometimes for days, weeks or even months. It can be linked to a specific situation; it could be caused by a past trauma; or you could feel anxious for no identifiable reason at all. When you're feeling anxious, there is a range of physical symptoms you might experience, including having a raised heart rate, feeling dizzy, being out of breath, or having tingling in your arms and legs. You might feel that you're out of control, or even worry that you're having a heart attack. Although these symptoms can be scary, it's important to remember that they will pass with time.

WHAT CAN I DO?

If you're prone to feeling anxious, there are plenty of things you can do to get yourself into a better frame of mind. In this book, you'll find techniques for staying calm, and simple tricks you can use to change the way you think. What's more, you will learn how to keep your mind and body in harmony with simple acts of self-care, such as eating well and sleeping deeply.

Part One:

RELEASE
YOURSELF FROM
ANXIETY

Optimism is the
faith that leads
to achievement;
nothing can be
done without hope.

Helen Keller

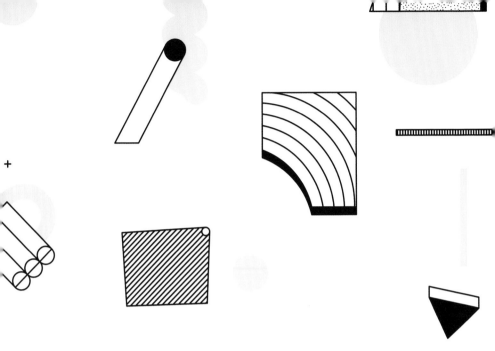

UNDERSTANDING
YOUR ANXIETY

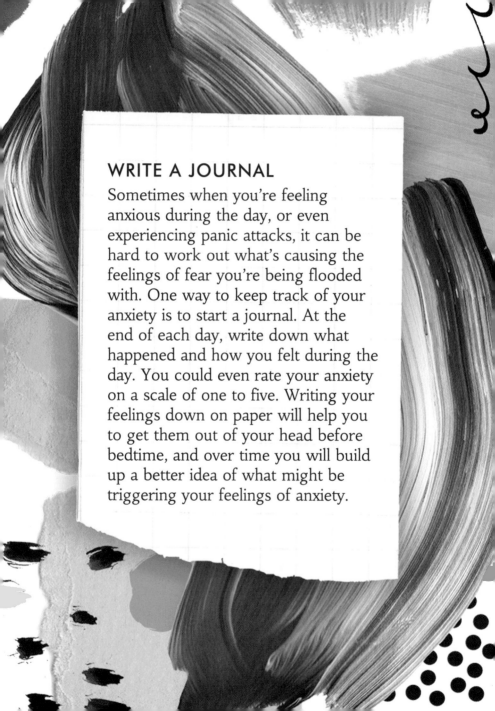

WRITE A JOURNAL

Sometimes when you're feeling anxious during the day, or even experiencing panic attacks, it can be hard to work out what's causing the feelings of fear you're being flooded with. One way to keep track of your anxiety is to start a journal. At the end of each day, write down what happened and how you felt during the day. You could even rate your anxiety on a scale of one to five. Writing your feelings down on paper will help you to get them out of your head before bedtime, and over time you will build up a better idea of what might be triggering your feelings of anxiety.

BE HONEST WITH YOURSELF

Sometimes a thought pops into your head which you'd rather not admit, even to yourself. But judging your thoughts or trying to push them away will only make things harder in the long run. Instead of trying to analyse what floats to the surface of your mind, simply accept your thoughts as fleeting feelings and move on.

IDENTIFY YOUR TRIGGERS

If you're feeling anxious, it can be helpful to try to work out what's triggering your feelings. Find a moment in your day when you can be alone without being interrupted by anyone. Reflect on the times when you felt most anxious over the last few days or weeks. Who were you with? What were you thinking about? What were your surroundings? It might help to write your feelings down, or you might prefer to keep them in your head. Do you notice a link between a certain person or situation and your feelings of anxiety? If so, that person or situation could be triggering your anxiousness.

KNOW YOUR GOALS

Think about the last time you achieved something that you'd set out to do. It could be handing in a report on time, going to an exercise class, or even popping to the shops to buy the things on your list. How did it feel? Probably pretty great. That's because one of the things that makes us tick as humans is setting goals and achieving them. While having unrealistic expectations of yourself can be damaging, setting yourself small goals can help to manage anxiety. This is because it gives us a sense of purpose. Spend a few minutes making a list of five small things you want to achieve this week. Display your list somewhere and tick them off as you complete them.

BE PATIENT

Working through anxiety can be a long process, and it's easy to feel frustrated with yourself if you can't immediately get to the bottom of what's making you feel a certain way. But it's important to be patient. Just take every day as it comes and trust that things will get better.

The journey of a thousand miles begins with a single step.

Lao Tzu

I will put myself first

CHANGE ONE THING

When you're feeling anxious, it's natural to want to curb your feelings by making changes to your lifestyle. While this can be helpful for reducing anxiety, changing too many things at once can actually make the problem worse. This is because too much change at once can destabilize your mood. If you're thinking about making big lifestyle changes, such as cutting certain foods out of your diet, or seeing a particular person less frequently, try to make only one change at a time. This way, you'll feel more able to cope with the change and you'll have a clearer picture of how that variable affects your anxiety.

GIVE YOURSELF SPACE

Talking to friends or family can be a good way of working through your anxiety, but remember that these are your own private thoughts. If you don't feel ready or able to share them with anyone else yet, you don't have to.

TIME IS PRECIOUS

It's hard to control feelings of anxiety, but remember that we all have a limited time to enjoy life. Are your worries really worth wasting precious minutes or hours of your life for? If not, then put them to one side.

UNDERSTANDING
TRIGGERS VERSUS CAUSES

Finding your triggers can be a useful step towards tackling anxiety, but it's important to know that triggers don't necessarily cause your anxiety – they simply set off the feelings of fear in your mind like a domino effect. This could be because of an association between the cause of your anxiety and the trigger in your mind – for example, if you're anxious about your job, receiving an email could trigger feelings of anxiety. Common causes of anxiety are genetics, financial stress, relationship worries or concerns about a health condition. Meanwhile, common triggers are having too much time alone to think, or spending time in certain places or with certain people.

TRY NOT TO CATASTROPHIZE

When everything seems to be going wrong, it's easy to imagine the absolute worst-case scenario. Everybody does it. In fact, it's a defence mechanism that our brains use to try to keep us safe. However, it can make your anxieties worse if you obsess about what might happen. Instead, allow yourself to think of the worst thing that could happen and then ask yourself what you would do to cope with that situation. Then put it to one side and try to move on. Don't let yourself start thinking about the worst-case scenario again.

REMEMBER THAT IT WON'T LAST FOR EVER

We all have times in our lives when we feel anxious, but whatever happens, anxiety doesn't last for ever. Next time you're feeling worried, try to bear in mind that in a few weeks or months you'll feel better. Let yourself move with the ebb and flow of life.

C. S. Lewis

TECHNIQUES FOR DEALING WITH ANXIETY

ACKNOWLEDGE YOUR TRIGGERS

One of the most effective ways to deal with whatever triggers your anxiety is to simply acknowledge the triggers' existence. When you discover a trigger, say to yourself: "This triggers anxious thoughts in my mind." Try not to judge the trigger or explain why it makes you feel anxious. Simply recognizing that it sets off negative emotions in your head will give the trigger less power over you in the future.

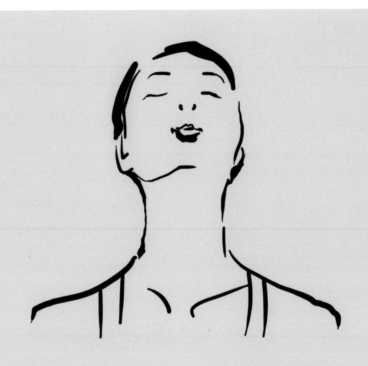

TAKE A DEEP BREATH

The next time you feel anxiety
rising in your chest, stop and take
a deep breath. Feel the air in your
lungs pushing your chest out, and
let the breath go down into your
stomach. Then push the air out
of your mouth until there is
nothing left. Do this five times
or until you start to feel calmer.

SURROUND YOURSELF WITH POSITIVE PEOPLE

Think about the last time you confided in a friend who was truly helpful and supportive. It's one of the best feelings in the world. But sadly not everyone we spend time with makes us feel supported and loved. Even with the best intentions, sometimes people let us down or have a hidden agenda.

Think about the people you spend time with on a day-to-day basis. Are they making you feel happy and supported or anxious and down?

Surround yourself with people who make you feel good about yourself, and minimize the time you spend with people who are a negative influence.

COUNT TO TEN

It's one of the oldest tricks in the book, and one of the most effective. When you feel anxiety or fear welling inside you, count slowly from one to ten in your head. Now think about whether you're still anxious or whether the feeling has subsided.

DO YOUR BEST

One of the most common causes of anxiety is the quest for perfection. We expect ourselves to do perfectly every time and get anxious when we fall short. Instead, fix your sights on doing the best you possibly can and accept that your best is good enough.

RESOLVE CONFLICTS

Nobody likes falling out with people. A common cause of anxiety is conflicts in relationships, be it with a romantic partner, family member, friend or colleague. If you're anxious about a conflict with someone, think about how you can resolve the situation. Would it help to sit down with this person and talk about your differences?
Do you need to speak to someone else about their behaviour, like a more senior colleague? Or, if the conflict can't be resolved, is it possible to minimize the amount of time you spend with this person? Whatever you decide, put some steps in place to stop the conflict from making you feel anxious.

i am

STRONGER

THan my

anxiety

ACCEPT WHAT YOU CAN'T CONTROL

Sometimes your anxiety might stem from something you can change, like a relationship that is making you unhappy or a job you dislike. But at other times, you might be anxious about things you can't do anything about, like the health of a loved one, what's going on in the news or even the weather. It's important to differentiate between the two. If you're anxious about something you have control over, think about what you can change to make the situation better. However, if you're feeling worried about something beyond your control, think about ways you can come to terms with the situation. Worrying about something you can't control will only make you feel worse.

BE GRATEFUL

You might have noticed that some people seem to be in good spirits no matter what life throws at them, while others seem to have it all but are still miserable. Gratitude could be the key to this – it makes you feel happy and fulfilled instead of anxious. Get into the habit of being grateful for everyday things, like someone making you a cup of tea or beautiful weather. Next time you find yourself getting into a spiral of worry, list three things you're grateful for. You may want to keep a gratitude journal, where you write down a few things that made you happy at the end of each day.

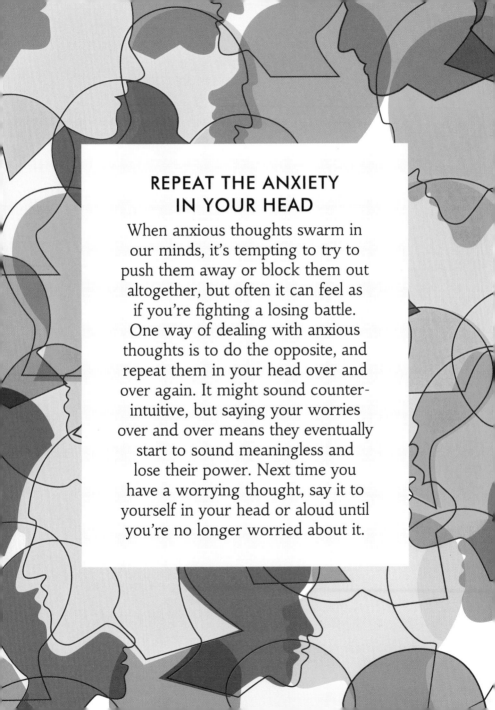

REPEAT THE ANXIETY IN YOUR HEAD

When anxious thoughts swarm in our minds, it's tempting to try to push them away or block them out altogether, but often it can feel as if you're fighting a losing battle. One way of dealing with anxious thoughts is to do the opposite, and repeat them in your head over and over again. It might sound counter-intuitive, but saying your worries over and over means they eventually start to sound meaningless and lose their power. Next time you have a worrying thought, say it to yourself in your head or aloud until you're no longer worried about it.

WATCH OUT FOR FALSE ALARMS

Sometimes the things which worry us are genuine
concerns, but other times we worry about things
that we know are very unlikely to happen, such
as leaving the cooker on or forgetting to lock the
door. When one of these worries pops into your
head, recognize it for what it is – a false alarm –
and don't allow yourself to get anxious about it.

TAKE TIME OUT

Be it work, school or family commitments, sometimes things get on top of us. If you're feeling anxious or overwhelmed, don't be afraid to take some time out of your day to go for a walk or catch up with a friend. You'll feel infinitely better for having a few minutes to yourself.

TALK TO SOMEONE

As the old adage goes, a problem shared is a problem halved. If you're struggling with anxiety, sometimes just voicing your thoughts aloud can make them seem less scary. You might realize that they're less serious than they appear when you're sitting alone thinking, or lying in bed at night. A good friend will acknowledge your problems without making you feel silly, and help you feel that you're not facing them alone. It might be enough for your friend just to listen, or between you, you may be able to think of simple steps to help you tackle your anxieties.

Start by doing what's

NECESSARY,

then do what's

POSSIBLE;

and suddenly you

are doing the

IMPOSSIBLE.

ANONYMOUS

Part two:

KEEPING WELL TO REDUCE ANXIETY

Setting goals is the first step in turning the invisible to the visible.

TONY ROBBINS

EATING WELL

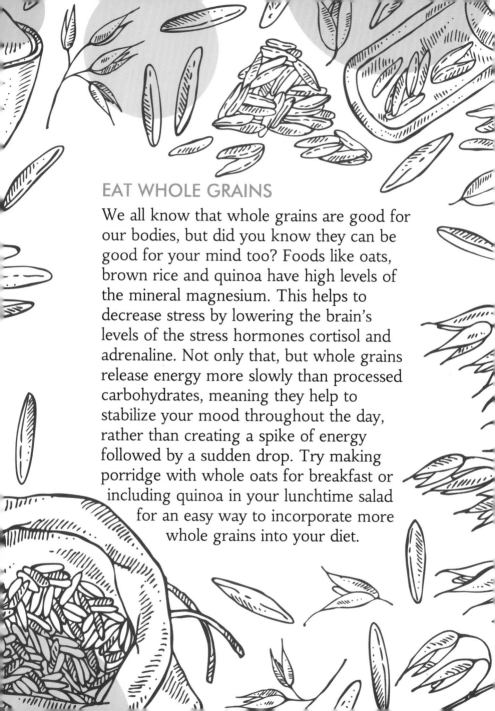

EAT WHOLE GRAINS

We all know that whole grains are good for our bodies, but did you know they can be good for your mind too? Foods like oats, brown rice and quinoa have high levels of the mineral magnesium. This helps to decrease stress by lowering the brain's levels of the stress hormones cortisol and adrenaline. Not only that, but whole grains release energy more slowly than processed carbohydrates, meaning they help to stabilize your mood throughout the day, rather than creating a spike of energy followed by a sudden drop. Try making porridge with whole oats for breakfast or including quinoa in your lunchtime salad for an easy way to incorporate more whole grains into your diet.

STAY HYDRATED

Water makes up 70 per cent of the human body and 85 per cent of your brain tissue. Drinking plenty of fresh water is important for maintaining a healthy mind. If you struggle to drink as much as you should, try keeping a bottle of water on your desk or in your bag to remind you to take a drink. You could also infuse your water with fruits, veggies or herbs for variety or if you don't like the taste of plain water – mint and cucumber is a particularly refreshing option.

Good food nourishes my body and mind

HAVE REGULAR MEALTIMES

When you're feeling anxious, it's easy to neglect basic self-care, like eating regularly. But having low blood sugar can cause you to feel jittery and nervous, making your anxieties seem even worse. Aim to eat three meals a day to even out your blood sugar throughout the day and help smooth out your mood.

DRINK HERBAL TEA

Sipping a warm drink is a great excuse to take a moment out of your day to reflect, and why not swap your usual coffee or builder's tea for a herbal tea for even more anxiety-busting benefits? Look for herbal teas that contain tulsi or holy basil; originating in India, this herb has been used for thousands of years to tackle stress and anxiety. This is because it causes the levels of the stress hormone cortisol to drop, meaning you'll feel calmer and more able to cope with stressful situations. At bedtime, sip teas with valerian root in, as this has a sedative effect.

EAT MINDFULLY

When you're anxious, it's easy to wolf down your food without thinking about it, but this can make you feel worse. Instead, take time to savour your food. Think about what every mouthful tastes like, and chew it carefully before swallowing. This will force your brain to focus on the present and forget about any worries.

GO EASY ON THE COFFEE

Many people can't imagine starting their day without a mug of steaming coffee in their hand. Not only does it boost your energy when you're feeling tired, but it kick-starts your metabolism too. While conventional wisdom says that people who suffer from anxiety should avoid caffeine, studies show that coffee in small doses can actually help tackle anxiety. This is because it helps the brain release dopamine, which can level your mood. Just be careful not to drink more than a few cups a day, as too much caffeine could leave you feeling jittery and on edge. This is especially true towards the end of the day, when it could stop you from getting that much-needed shut-eye.

BEWARE OF SWEET TREATS

It's easy to reach for sugary foods like biscuits or chocolate when you're feeling anxious, but while they might give you a small boost in the short term, in the long term they'll leave you feeling worse. This is because sugar gives you a short spike of energy, followed by a drop that will lower your mood. Instead opt for foods that release energy slowly, like fruit, veg and whole grains.

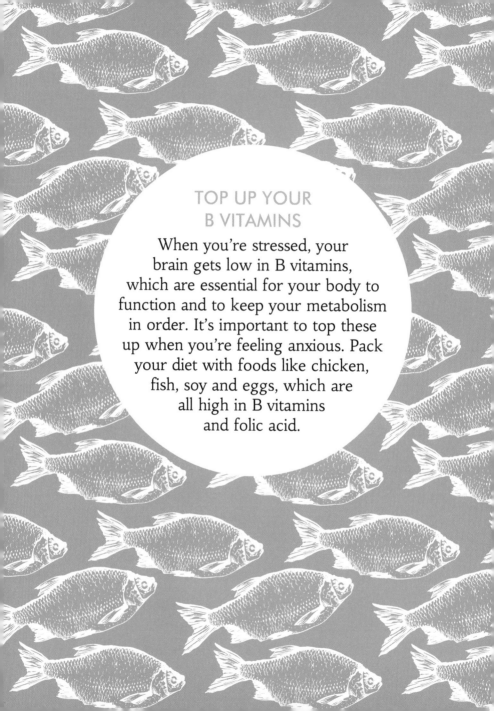

TOP UP YOUR
B VITAMINS

When you're stressed, your
brain gets low in B vitamins,
which are essential for your body to
function and to keep your metabolism
in order. It's important to top these
up when you're feeling anxious. Pack
your diet with foods like chicken,
fish, soy and eggs, which are
all high in B vitamins
and folic acid.

EAT YOUR WAY TO A *calmer mind*

STOP WINE O'CLOCK

When anxiety hits, it can be tempting to reach for a glass of wine or a pint of beer to soothe your stresses. But while there's nothing wrong with the occasional drink, drinking too much alcohol can deepen your anxiety. Have you ever noticed that you often feel down or anxious after a big night of drinking? This is because alcohol lowers levels of the happy hormone serotonin, meaning you're more likely to feel low after a session of heavy drinking. What's more, it puts your nervous system on high alert in order to counter the sedative effects of alcohol, meaning you will sleep less deeply and may feel on edge. Plan alcohol-free days during your week, and switch to drinking non-alcoholic drinks after a certain time of night. You can always order tonic water with a slice of lemon – nobody will know there's no gin in your glass.

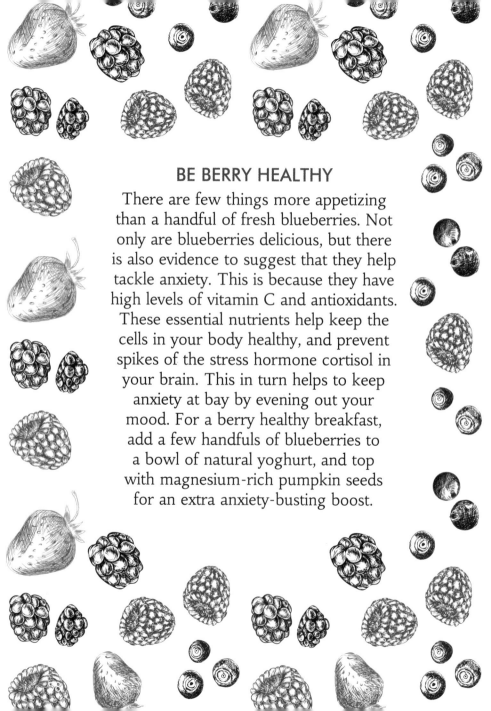

BE BERRY HEALTHY

There are few things more appetizing than a handful of fresh blueberries. Not only are blueberries delicious, but there is also evidence to suggest that they help tackle anxiety. This is because they have high levels of vitamin C and antioxidants. These essential nutrients help keep the cells in your body healthy, and prevent spikes of the stress hormone cortisol in your brain. This in turn helps to keep anxiety at bay by evening out your mood. For a berry healthy breakfast, add a few handfuls of blueberries to a bowl of natural yoghurt, and top with magnesium-rich pumpkin seeds for an extra anxiety-busting boost.

THE MAGIC MINERAL

When it comes to keeping anxiety at bay, there's one nutrient that is crucial. The mineral magnesium is a magic ingredient for fighting anxiety as it helps to lower levels of the stress hormones cortisol and adrenaline in the brain. When you're feeling stressed, your levels of magnesium become low. This means it's especially important to eat a diet rich in magnesium when you're feeling anxious to replenish your stores of the mineral. Foods like nuts, whole grains, spinach, pumpkin seeds, chickpeas and avocado are naturally high in stress-beating magnesium, and it is also found in meat and fish.

One cannot *think well, love well, sleep well,* if one has not *dined well.*

VIRGINIA WOOLF

EXERCISING TO HELP YOUR MIND

CENTRE YOURSELF

One of the best things about exercising is that it helps to focus your mind. Before exercising, take inspiration from the Japanese martial art of aikido and centre yourself. First, take a few deep breaths and allow your lungs to fill up with air. Concentrate on the physical sensations of breathing. Next, find your centre of gravity, about two inches below your belly button, and concentrate on that. Imagine sending all your thoughts and feelings to your centre of gravity. As you inhale, imagine breathing in positive thoughts, and as you exhale, imagine letting go of any anxiety or negative thoughts.

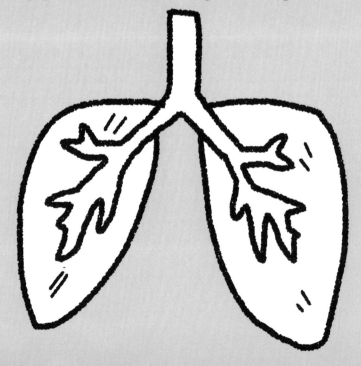

GET OUT AND ABOUT

When we think of doing exercise, we often imagine going to the gym, but exercising outside can provide an extra anxiety-busting boost to your workout. Why not swap your gym routine or online exercise video for a jog in your local park? Take in the sights, sounds and smells of nature as you exercise, and notice how much better you feel.

BE A YOGI

People often assume that in order to do yoga you have to be flexible, but in fact it's a practice that almost anyone can try. Many yoga classes combine a series of poses with deep breathing and meditation. This combination can be great for reducing anxiety in the short term, and practising it every day has been proven to lower anxiety levels in the long term too. Start by learning child's pose. Sit on your exercise or yoga mat with your buttocks resting on your heels and your knees apart. Lean your body down so your chest is as close to the ground as possible, and stretch your hands out on the ground in front of you. This relieves tension in the neck and shoulders and will make you feel instantly calmer.

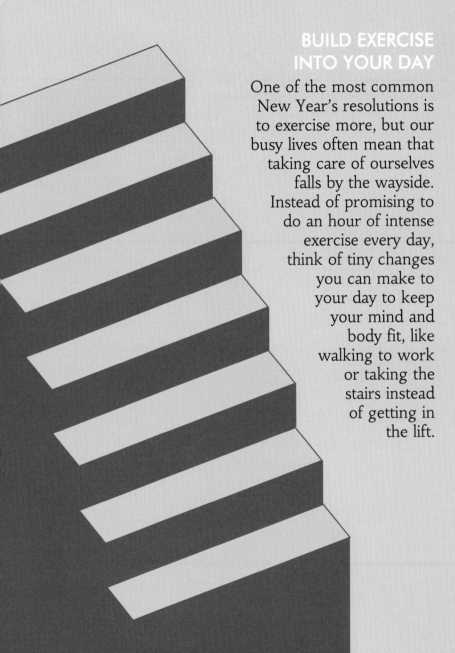

BUILD EXERCISE INTO YOUR DAY

One of the most common New Year's resolutions is to exercise more, but our busy lives often mean that taking care of ourselves falls by the wayside. Instead of promising to do an hour of intense exercise every day, think of tiny changes you can make to your day to keep your mind and body fit, like walking to work or taking the stairs instead of getting in the lift.

BOOST YOUR SELF-ESTEEM THROUGH EXERCISE

Getting fit doesn't just benefit your body: studies show that people who exercise regularly have higher self-esteem, more self-control and feel more able to rise to any challenges they may face. Furthermore, a good workout boosts your energy levels, releases feel-good endorphins and makes you feel great. Ever heard the phrase "nobody ever regretted a workout"? It's true! So why not give it a go?

i WILL MOVE MY BODY

to still my mind

RUN FOR IT

You might have heard of the term "runner's high" – the natural rush of positivity some people feel after they've been for a run. Like all forms of exercise, running floods the brain with the happy hormone serotonin and endorphins, which boost your mood. Even after the high is over, running can help you sleep more deeply and generally feel calmer. Why is running particularly good for beating anxiety and depression? Some people think it's because running is rhythmic, helping you to get into a meditative state of mind. Try going for a gentle jog and feel your mood improve.

TRY TEAM SPORTS

While some people prefer
to exercise alone, trying a new
sport can be a good way to meet
other people. Studies show that those
who play team sports feel happier than
those who exercise on their own, due
to the social bonds they form. Join a local
netball or football club and give it a go.

PRACTISE T'AI CHI

It might not be the first thing that springs to your mind when you're stressed, but studies show that the ancient Chinese practice of t'ai chi could help relieve anxiety and depression. Like yoga, t'ai chi combines gentle exercise with deep breathing and meditation, which help to soothe the mind and body. It involves a series of slow, controlled movements that flow into one another so the body is constantly moving. The idea is to help the 'energy of life' flow easily through the body. Why not find a local t'ai chi group or follow online videos to learn the basic poses and sequences?

GO FOR A WALK

If you don't exercise often, starting
a sport or fitness trend can be
intimidating, but even going for
a short walk can help clear your
mind and boost your mood. Take
a 10-minute walk every day and
see how much better you feel.

MOVE YOUR BODY

Exercise is great for your mental health, but you don't have to play sport to feel the psychological benefits. In modern life, many of us spend a large portion of the day sitting down, be it behind a desk, at the wheel of a car or on the sofa. A simple lifestyle change that will make a big difference to how you feel is to ensure you keep moving throughout the day. If you have to sit down for a long period of time, make sure you take a break every hour to move your body. You could go for a short walk or simply stand up and stretch out your neck and shoulders.

STRETCH

When you're anxious, tension often
builds up in your muscles, especially
around the neck and shoulders.
Try standing with your back against
a wall and gradually rolling your head
and neck down towards your feet
until only your backside is against
the wall. Let yourself hang there and
feel the tension drain away. Then
roll slowly back up to standing.

DANCE LIKE NO ONE IS WATCHING

When was the last time you danced with wild abandon? How did it make you feel? It's something we often do as children, but as we get older, we tend to dance less and less. But taking up dancing is one of the best forms of exercise for beating anxiety. That's because it combines the mood-boosting power of music with the stress-busting impact of moving your body. The best thing is, you don't need to go to a class or workshop to dance: all you need to do is play some tunes in your bedroom and have a boogie.

The fastest
way to still
the mind
is to move
the body.

GABRIELLE ROTH

SLEEPING WELL

CREATE A SLEEP SANCTUARY

Whether it's working, watching TV or scrolling through social media, our beds often become a place where we do anything but sleep. When bedtime arrives, it can then be a struggle to drift off. This is because our brains create an association between our beds and being awake, meaning sleep can sometimes become elusive. Insomnia can make anxiety worse, so make sure you get a restful night by banning everything but sleep and sex from the bedroom. Resist the temptation to eat breakfast or work late wrapped up in your duvet, and stick to other rooms in the house. Then when you get into bed, your brain will automatically switch into resting mode.

KEEP COOL

Keeping cool during the night is essential
for a good kip, as being too hot will mean
you wake up more frequently. Try switching
polyester sheets for cotton ones, which are
more breathable, and keep a window open
during warm nights if it's safe to do so.

STICK TO A CONSISTENT SLEEP ROUTINE

While weekend lie-ins feel like a treat, they can disrupt your sleep pattern, meaning you struggle to fall asleep again in the evening. Instead of getting sleep deprived during the week and bingeing at the weekend, aim to get around eight hours' sleep each night, and wake up at roughly the same time each morning.

MIND YOUR WORRIES

We've all had nights where we lie awake tossing and turning without getting a wink of sleep. And when you're feeling anxious, it's easy to get distracted by turning over your problems in your mind before bed. Break the habit of overthinking late at night by using mindfulness techniques. Focus on the physical sensations of being in bed. Think about the warmth of being under the duvet, the softness of the sheets against your skin, and the weight of your body pressing down on the mattress. Breathe in deeply and feel your chest expanding, and when you exhale, focus on how your body softens.

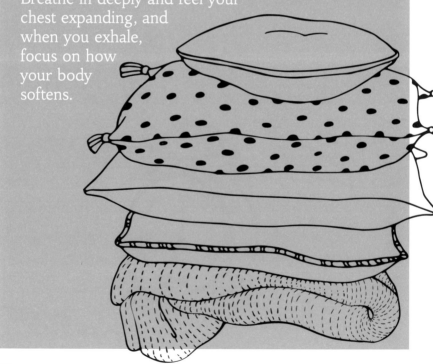

DO A DIGITAL DETOX

Whether it's watching the news, or comparing ourselves to others on social media, there are lots of ways that looking at a screen can induce anxiety. What's more, the blue light emitted from screens prevents your brain from going to sleep. Try banning tech from the bedroom or putting your phone to charge on the other side of the room at night.

WIND DOWN

With so much to do during the day, it's tempting to collapse straight into bed without a moment's thought. But going straight to bed after a long day can mean you get a bad night's sleep. This is because any anxieties from earlier will still be whirling around your head, making it difficult to relax. Experts recommend creating a bedtime routine, similar to the one you might have had as a child. First, get into your pyjamas and clean your teeth, as doing this later on can wake you up again. Next, let your brain unwind by reading a book or listening to a podcast for a few minutes before going to sleep – anything relaxing that doesn't involve looking at a screen is ideal.

IF YOU WAKE UP, GET UP

Waking up during the night can be frustrating, especially as it often takes a long time to get back to sleep. And the longer you go without drifting off again, the more anxious you can feel about being tired the following day. Rather than lying awake staring at the ceiling, next time you wake up in the middle of the night, try getting out of bed to get a glass of water or go to the toilet. The simple action of getting out of bed breaks the repetitive thought cycle of not sleeping and becoming frustrated. This means that when you do climb back under the covers, it's easier to fall asleep again.

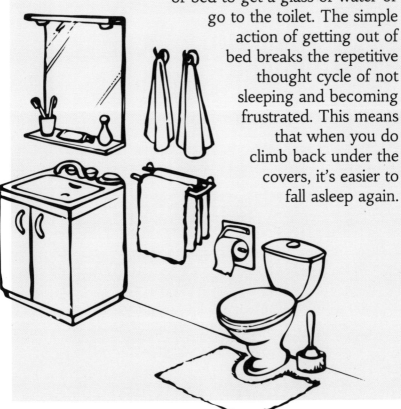

TAKE A WARM BATH

We often associate bedtime with feeling
warm and cosy, but in fact your body
temperature needs to drop slightly
in order for you to get off to sleep.
Try having a warm bath or shower
before bed. Your temperature will drop
when you get out, making it easier
to snooze when you climb into bed.

FIGHT THE URGE TO NAP

When your anxieties are keeping you awake at night, napping during the day can seem like the answer. In fact, taking naps in the afternoon can sabotage your sleep later on in the evening. This is because it disrupts your sleep cycle, making it harder to drift off later in the day. If you feel like having a nap, why not go for a walk or call a friend to take your mind off the tiredness? If you really do need some sleep, restrict your nap to 20 minutes, and when the 20-minute window is up, be strict with yourself and get out of bed.

DIM THE LIGHTS

If you can, swap the harsh glare
of an overhead light for the warm
glow of a bedside lamp before
you go to sleep. Dimming the
lights will help signal to your brain
that it's time to go to sleep,
meaning you'll begin to
wind down and relax.

SLEEP MINDFULLY

If you struggle to fall asleep, try using mindfulness techniques. Lie in a comfortable position and close your eyes. Take a deep breath through your nose for five counts, then breathe out through your mouth for seven counts. Put one hand on your stomach and feel it rise and fall with each breath. Focus on how the bedclothes feel. Are they soft? Do you feel warm? Which parts of your body support your weight on the mattress? If any thoughts come into your head while you do this exercise, try to watch them float past like balloons rather than holding on to them.

Sleep is
the best
meditation.

DALAI LAMA

Part three:

LET YOURSELF GO

IT ALL BEGINS
AND ENDS IN
YOUR MIND.
WHAT YOU
GIVE POWER
TO HAS
POWER OVER
YOU, IF YOU
ALLOW IT.

LEON BROWN

RELAXATION
TECHNIQUES

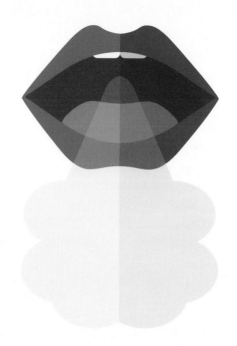

BREATHE DEEPLY

Take a deep breath. It's a phrase we hear so often that it's become a cliché, but deep breathing is a very effective way of relaxing your mind and body when you feel anxious. This is because when you're stressed, your body goes into "fight or flight" mode as it prepares to tackle a physical threat. Your heart rate increases, your breathing becomes shallower and your pupils dilate. By filling your lungs with a big, deep breath, you interrupt this process and help put your body back into resting mode. The next time you start to feel anxious, take a long breath through your nose and push the air out through your mouth. Do this as many times as you need to before you start to feel better.

PUT YOUR FEET UP

We all like to put our feet up at the end of a long day, but did you know that elevating your feet can actually help you feel less anxious? When you're stressed, blood is pumped to the feet because of the "fight or flight" response, but putting them up signals to your body that it's time to relax again. Try stretching out on the sofa with your feet resting on the arm and take a few deep breaths.

NOW IS THE TIME TO FEEL GOOD

BE OPEN-MINDED

We all have days when we struggle
to relax, even when using relaxation
techniques, but it's important to remain
open-minded. The quickest way to
stop yourself from relaxing is to tell
yourself that a certain technique won't
make you feel any better. Just give it a
go! Try out different techniques until
you find what works best for you.

FIND YOUR HAPPY PLACE

Think of a place where you feel truly relaxed and at home. It could be your bedroom, a family member's house or somewhere you've been on holiday. Now imagine how you feel when you're there. Transporting yourself back to that place in your mind when you're anxious is a great way to relax. Next time you start to feel worried, find a comfortable spot and close your eyes. Imagine being in the place you just pictured. What can you see there? What can you hear? What can you smell and taste? Are you sitting or standing? What can you feel around you? Do this for 10 minutes or until you feel calmer.

SEND NEGATIVITY AWAY

We all have gloomy thoughts that cloud our brains from time to time. The trick is not to let them get on top of you. The next time you start thinking in a pessimistic way, imagine turning the negative thought into an object, like a ball, and then throwing it away. With practice, your mind will learn not to dwell on negative thoughts and you'll feel calmer.

GO CRAZY

Being anxious can create a lot of excess energy, so sometimes, in order to relax, we need to do the opposite and go a bit crazy. Whenever you're feeling stressed, try running around and waving your arms in the air, or putting on an upbeat song and dancing like crazy. You might feel silly at first, but soon all your anxiety will be flung off.

AND RELAX...

A good way to break anxious thought patterns is with a muscle-relaxing exercise. This involves tensing and relaxing different muscle groups in turn, until you've paid attention to every muscle in your body. Not only does it help you to get out of your own head, but with time it helps you recognize feelings of tension that might arise in your body during the day so you can relax the muscles again. Find a comfortable position and start by tensing all the muscles in one foot and then relax them again. Do this for your other foot, then move on to your calves, thighs and so on, until you've tensed every muscle from toe to head. You'll feel instantly calmer and more relaxed.

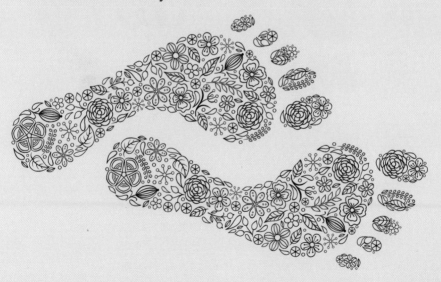

BE CREATIVE

Not everyone sees themselves as a brilliant
artist, but everyone is creative, and creating
something is a brilliant way to soothe anxieties.
The next time you're feeling stressed, why
not start a drawing, painting or craft project?
Don't focus on the end result – just enjoy
the process of creating something.

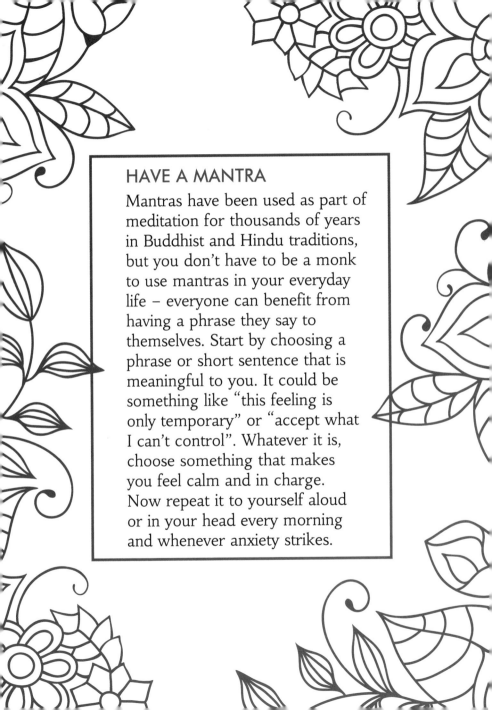

HAVE A MANTRA

Mantras have been used as part of meditation for thousands of years in Buddhist and Hindu traditions, but you don't have to be a monk to use mantras in your everyday life – everyone can benefit from having a phrase they say to themselves. Start by choosing a phrase or short sentence that is meaningful to you. It could be something like "this feeling is only temporary" or "accept what I can't control". Whatever it is, choose something that makes you feel calm and in charge. Now repeat it to yourself aloud or in your head every morning and whenever anxiety strikes.

I WILL
FACE MY
FEARS

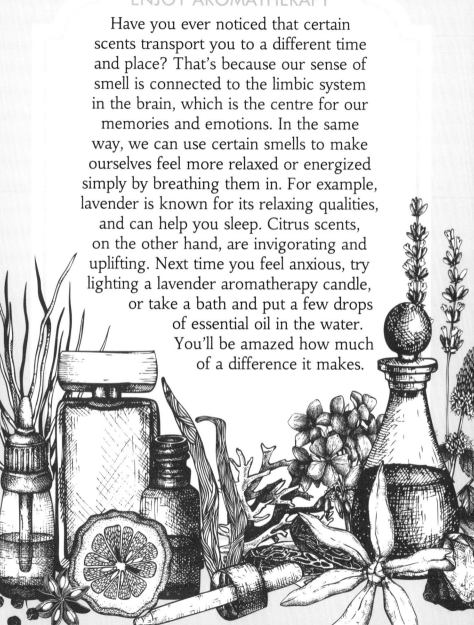

ENJOY AROMATHERAPY

Have you ever noticed that certain scents transport you to a different time and place? That's because our sense of smell is connected to the limbic system in the brain, which is the centre for our memories and emotions. In the same way, we can use certain smells to make ourselves feel more relaxed or energized simply by breathing them in. For example, lavender is known for its relaxing qualities, and can help you sleep. Citrus scents, on the other hand, are invigorating and uplifting. Next time you feel anxious, try lighting a lavender aromatherapy candle, or take a bath and put a few drops of essential oil in the water. You'll be amazed how much of a difference it makes.

RECOGNIZE THAT YOU'RE PANICKING

Sometimes when we're feeling anxious, we try to distract ourselves or make our worries seem smaller. But one of the most effective ways of getting through an anxious moment is to recognize your feelings. Say to yourself, "I'm feeling very anxious", and you'll start to feel calmer and more in control.

I'm feeling very anxious

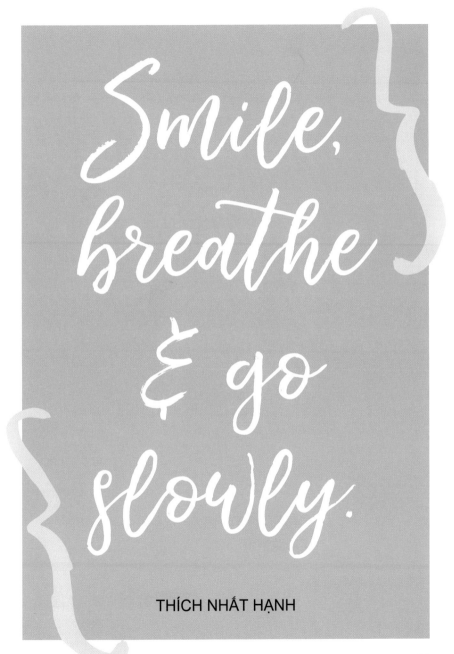

Smile, breathe & go slowly.

THÍCH NHẤT HẠNH

DE-STRESSING
TECHNIQUES

TAKE A SCREEN BREAK

Staring at a screen for long periods can feed anxiety because there are often multiple things demanding your attention at once – like an email notification, a pop-up advert or a text message from a friend. All of these things require your brain to make tiny decisions about what to deal with first, which can leave you feeling exhausted and stressed. Aim to spend at least a few minutes every day relaxing without looking at your phone, computer or TV. You'll be amazed how much more grounded you feel, and even after a few minutes your energy will be renewed.

HUG SOMEONE

There are few things more comforting than being enveloped in a hug. And it turns out that hugs don't just feel good – they also release endorphins in your brain that boost your mood and relieve stress. So why not hug away your worries?

PHONE A FRIEND

Sometimes a few comforting words
from a friend are all you need to
make your worries fade away.
Just hearing a familiar voice can
make you feel instantly better
– it doesn't necessarily matter
what you talk about. If you're
feeling stressed, try phoning
a friend for a quick chat.

GIVE YOURSELF A HAND (MASSAGE)

When people are stressed, they tend to wring their hands, and it turns out this is more than just a habit. Massaging certain areas of your hands can help to relieve stress, according to reflexology practitioners – the muscles in the hands connect to other areas in the body, and relaxing the correlating parts of the hands can effect a physical change on the body as a whole. Next time you're feeling tense, place your thumb on the squishy part of the hand between your other thumb and index finger and rub in a circular motion for 10–15 seconds. Then take your thumb and firmly rub the top part of the little finger from the top knuckle towards the top of the finger for another 10–15 seconds. These exercises help to calm the mind.

i WiLL REMEMBER tO COUNT MY BLESSiNGS

GET AWAY

Sometimes the routine of daily life can get you down. Every so often it's good to break up your routine by going somewhere new or doing something different. Why not plan a holiday or short break to help relieve your stresses? If you can't get away for a full-on holiday, why not hop on a train for a day trip to a nearby but unexplored town? You could even have a weekend "minibreak" from the comfort of your own home: hide away all your gadgets and anything that reminds you of your daily routine or work, and have a pampering, relaxing weekend of reading good books, going for walks around your town as if you were a tourist seeing everything for the first time, and cooking yourself up some delicious foods that remind you of your favourite place.

BE STILL

In our busy modern lives we always seem to be in a rush, whether we're trying to get to work on time, meeting a friend, or whipping up a quick dinner. It's rare to have a moment of stillness and quiet, but it could be exactly what we need to help us to relax. No matter how frantic your day is, try to take 10 minutes alone to be truly still. You might want to sit on a park bench and shut your eyes, or simply close the door to your bedroom when you get home and sit on your bed for a moment. Even if it means locking yourself in the bathroom for 10 minutes, try to find time to be still every day.

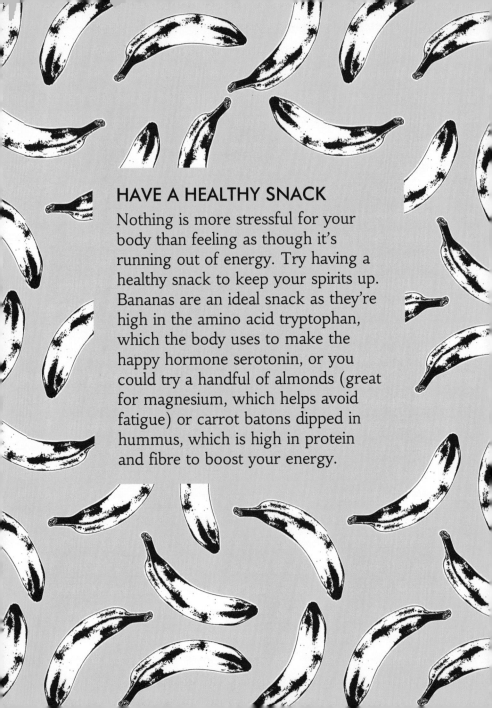

HAVE A HEALTHY SNACK

Nothing is more stressful for your body than feeling as though it's running out of energy. Try having a healthy snack to keep your spirits up. Bananas are an ideal snack as they're high in the amino acid tryptophan, which the body uses to make the happy hormone serotonin, or you could try a handful of almonds (great for magnesium, which helps avoid fatigue) or carrot batons dipped in hummus, which is high in protein and fibre to boost your energy.

BLOCK OUT YOUR CALENDAR

It's stressful failing to reach a meeting on time or
running for a train when you know you're going
to be late. But all too often we're tempted to stay
an extra few minutes at work, or plan to see two
friends back to back in order to keep everyone
happy. The result is we often end up scrambling
from A to B in a daze of stress. But it doesn't
have to be that way. One simple trick you can use
to de-stress is to block out an extra 10 minutes
in your calendar for travelling time or potential
delays whenever you have somewhere to be.
This tiny change will ensure you arrive on time,
feeling fresh and prepared instead of flustered.

START A HOBBY

The older we get, the more our hobbies
are neglected in favour of working and seeing
friends. But having something you do purely
for enjoyment can have huge benefits for
your mental health. Doing something you
love regularly gives you something to look
forward to and a sense of achievement.
Try taking up a new class or fitness
challenge, and see how much
better you feel.

SMILE

It might be the last thing you want to do if you're feeling stressed, but smiling can help relieve tension and encourage your mind to unwind. Studies show that people doing difficult tasks whilst smiling had a lower heart rate and felt less stressed than those doing the same tasks with a neutral expression. Scientists believe that smiling lowers the brain's levels of the stress hormone cortisol, making you feel less anxious. It doesn't seem to matter whether the smile is genuine or fake – just moving the facial muscles is enough to feel the benefits. So next time you're feeling down, try to grin and bear it.

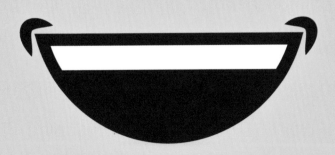

A SMILE IS A CURVE THAT SETS

EVERYTHING
STRAIGHT.

PHYLLIS DILLER

DON'T COMPARE

Whether it's your friends, family, or people you work with, it's easy to compare yourself to others because it's our nature as human beings to want to know how we're doing in comparison to everyone else. Modern life kicks our comparison habits into overdrive, as we're bombarded with images from adverts and social media that seem to make our lives look dull and unsatisfying. These constant comparisons can make us feel anxious that we're not living up to the high expectations we set for ourselves. Try to get out of the comparison trap and be happy with the life you're living. Remember: what you see in adverts and social media doesn't always reflect reality.

The world
only exists in
your eyes...

You can make it
as big or as small
as you want

Being Kind to Yourself

TALK TO YOURSELF LIKE YOU WOULD A FRIEND

Whether or not we like to admit it, we all talk to ourselves throughout the day. Although we might not do it aloud, there's often a running commentary going on in our minds. We say things like "Why did I miss the bus? That was silly" or "I can't believe I forgot my lunchbox again". Sadly, many of the things we say to ourselves are negative. A lot of the time, we wouldn't stand for the way we talk to ourselves if it was a friend saying those things to us constantly. Talk to yourself in the same way you would talk to your best friend. Instead of being critical, try to be encouraging.

I WILL BE A FRIEND, NOT AN ENEMY, TO MYSELF

SOAK YOUR TROUBLES AWAY

If you're feeling stressed, shut the
bathroom door and run yourself a bath.
You might want to light a few candles, have
something nice to eat or drink, or put on
some relaxing music. You could even use
aromatherapy oils to help you unwind.

TO·DO LIST

_____

_____

_____

_____

_____

_____

_____

_____

DON'T BE A SHOULD-ER

We all have things we should do, whether it's taking out the rubbish, or preparing for a big day at work or school. But if we're not careful, the things we "should" be doing take over our lives. We make social arrangements because we feel we should keep up with a particular friend, even though they don't always make us feel good. Or we set impossible lists of things we think we should do, and then get upset when we don't get through them all. Next time you find yourself thinking that you should do something, ask yourself if you really need to, or if you're just doing it to please someone else. If you don't really need to do it, then don't.

PAT YOURSELF ON THE BACK

You might remember being told to pat yourself on the back at school, but it's something we get out of the habit of doing as adults. Instead we let our achievements go by unnoticed, and focus on the things we don't do so well at. After a while, this habit of ignoring our accomplishments can weigh us down and make us feel anxious. Next time you do something you're proud of, take a moment to congratulate yourself and give yourself a mental pat on the back. You could even start a journal and list things you've done each day which you feel proud of.

TREAT YOURSELF

Although going on a huge shopping spree is never a good way to manage anxiety, there's absolutely nothing wrong with treating yourself occasionally. It could be buying yourself a nice cup of coffee or a new candle for your room. Whatever it is, remember to treat yourself every once in a while.

PRACTISE SELF-FORGIVENESS

We all have things in life that we regret doing or saying, but holding on to these regrets can make us feel anxious. Take a moment to think about the things you wish you'd never done or said. Have you truly forgiven yourself for them, or are you still giving yourself a hard time over them? If it's the latter, remember that there's nothing you can do to change the past and instead try to move forward. You could write down your regrets on a piece of paper and burn it or throw it in the bin to symbolize that you've moved on. Or you could say aloud: "I forgive myself for what I did."

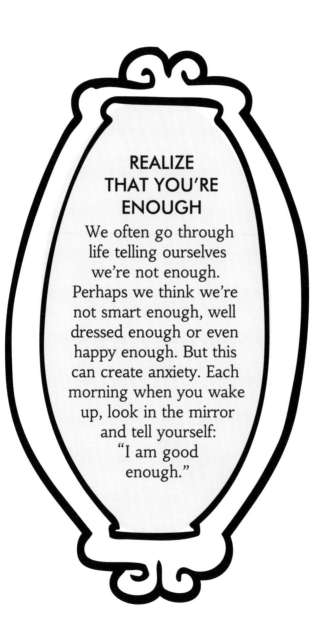

REALIZE THAT YOU'RE ENOUGH

We often go through life telling ourselves we're not enough. Perhaps we think we're not smart enough, well dressed enough or even happy enough. But this can create anxiety. Each morning when you wake up, look in the mirror and tell yourself: "I am good enough."

BE SELFISH

Often when someone is described as "selfish", the word is used in a negative way, but there's nothing wrong with being a little selfish from time to time. Instead of spending every single day trying to please others, remind yourself that sometimes it's okay to follow your heart and do the things you want to do.

INVEST TIME IN YOURSELF

If we had a friend who never bothered to spend quality time with us, we'd become annoyed and after a while the relationship would fizzle out. But for some reason, we often treat ourselves in a way we'd never accept from others. When was the last time you spent some quality time with yourself? It could be reading a book, having a bubble bath or going on a run – doing something just for you. If it was ages ago, think about ways you can build more "me time" into your day. It doesn't need to be hours – even 10 minutes at the beginning or end of each day will strengthen your relationship with yourself.

"ME TIME" IS TIME WELL SPENT

BEWARE
OF HIGH EXPECTATIONS

It's great to have goals in life, but sometimes having too high expectations of ourselves can make us feel anxious. Think about the things you're striving for at the moment. Are you aiming high or trying to do the impossible? Try to manage your expectations of yourself and instead aim for smaller, achievable goals that will keep you feeling positive.

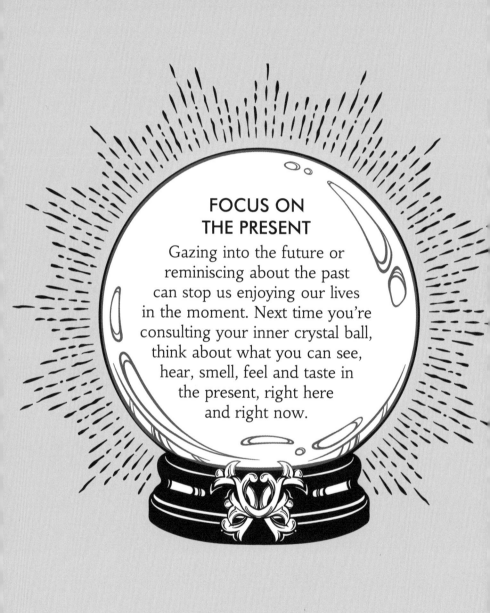

FOCUS ON
THE PRESENT

Gazing into the future or
reminiscing about the past
can stop us enjoying our lives
in the moment. Next time you're
consulting your inner crystal ball,
think about what you can see,
hear, smell, feel and taste in
the present, right here
and right now.

KNOWING YOURSELF IS THE

BEGINNING OF ALL WISDOM.

ARISTOTLE

Part four:

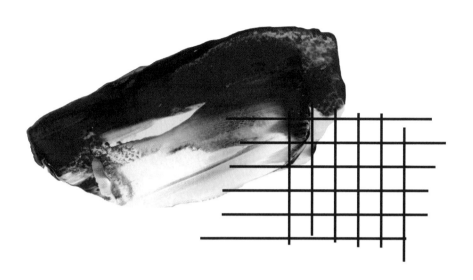

TACKLING ANXIETY FROM A PROFESSIONAL PERSPECTIVE

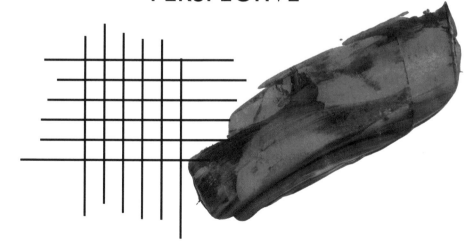

SOMETIMES THE SMALLEST STEP IN THE RIGHT DIRECTION ENDS UP BEING THE BIGGEST STEP OF YOUR LIFE.

ANONYMOUS

THERAPIES AND TREATMENTS

WHEN TO GET HELP

Everyone experiences feelings of anxiety from time to time, and it can be difficult to know whether to seek professional help or to try to manage the symptoms yourself. However, if you've noticed changes in the way you think and feel over the past few weeks or months and you're distressed about it, it might be worth speaking to a professional. This is especially true if you feel your mental health is having a negative impact on your day-to-day life. For example, if it's stopping you from doing things you would normally do, or preventing you from enjoying things you would normally like doing. There are treatments that you can try in the comfort of your own home, while others require you to seek professional help.

ASK YOURSELF WHAT YOU WANT

Before trying any kind of treatment or therapy, it's important to ask yourself what you want to get out of it. Do you want to feel instantly calmer? Or to get to the root of your problems? Perhaps you want to know how to deal with a specific situation or event. Whatever it is, be honest about what you want from the very beginning.

BE PREPARED TO HELP YOURSELF

A lot of people come to therapy expecting a magic cure. In reality, having therapy can be hard work and emotionally exhausting. If you take the route of therapy, you need to be prepared to work hard and perhaps face some difficult truths if you want to start feeling better.

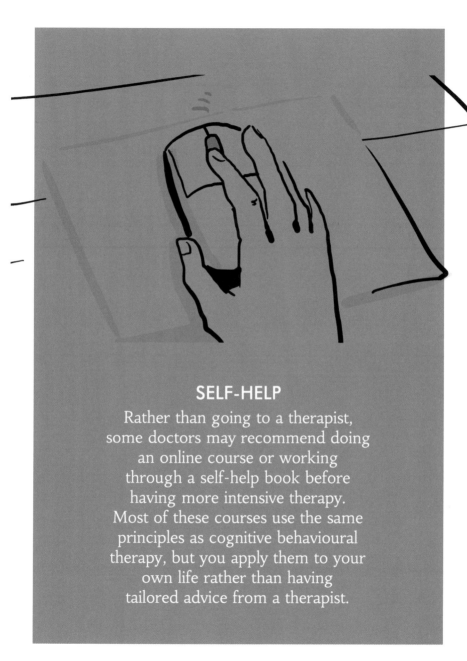

SELF-HELP

Rather than going to a therapist,
some doctors may recommend doing
an online course or working
through a self-help book before
having more intensive therapy.
Most of these courses use the same
principles as cognitive behavioural
therapy, but you apply them to your
own life rather than having
tailored advice from a therapist.

It's a sign of strength, not weakness, to ask for help

COGNITIVE BEHAVIOURAL THERAPY

One of the most common ways to treat anxiety is with cognitive behavioural therapy, often referred to as CBT. This type of therapy is a talking therapy, and involves working through your problems with a therapist. Unlike other types of psychotherapy, it doesn't focus on events in your past which could have caused the anxiety. Instead it focuses on your current thought patterns and how you can stop them from impacting your life. In particular, it tries to prevent you getting trapped in a cycle of negative thoughts. Rather than being given solutions, you and the therapist will work together to find the best way of treating the anxiety.

EXPOSURE THERAPY

A common type of cognitive behavioural therapy is exposure therapy, which is particularly helpful for people suffering from phobias or obsessive compulsive disorders (OCD). With the help of a therapist, you will be gradually exposed to the things you're scared of, and gradually you'll become less fearful.

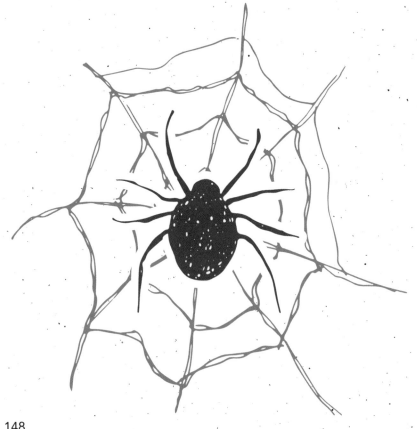

APPLIED RELAXATION

Applied relaxation is a technique some therapists teach to help you get through moments of panic. It involves learning to relax the muscles in the body individually to help you feel calmer. You may need to practise a few times to get the hang of it. Once you've learnt how to do this, you can use the technique to help you stay calm the next time a stressful situation arises, and maintain that feeling of calm throughout the day.

OBSERVE THE WORLD AROUND YOU

One of the simplest techniques therapists use is to help you take more notice of the world around you, and pay less attention to the thoughts swirling around your brain. Next time you're feeling anxious, take a moment to think about your surroundings. Where are you? What can you see, hear and smell? Do you taste anything? What can you feel? This will help you get out of the spiral of thoughts in your mind and feel calmer.

DON'T BE AFRAID TO EXPLORE DIFFERENT OPTIONS

Having treatment for anxiety can be daunting, especially if you haven't experienced therapy before. You should always give therapy a fair chance, but if you feel it's not working for you, don't be afraid to speak up. Remember that no two people are the same, and no two people will react in the exact same way to therapy. It could be that you need to speak to a different therapist or try a different technique to find what is most effective for you.

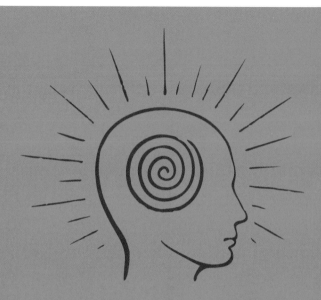

HYPNOSIS

Have you ever reached your front door and realized
the walk home seemed to pass in an instant? Or
peered into a mug and discovered you've drunk
the tea in it without noticing? When that happens,
it's because our brains have slipped into a state of
hypnosis, which we might call "being on autopilot".
In hypnotherapy, the therapist helps you relax
into this state so the conscious, critical part of
your mind switches off. Then they speak to the
unconscious part of your brain using repetitive
phrases and key words. For some people, this
can help tackle feelings of anxiety, or treat the
root cause. (Never attempt to hypnotize yourself
– instead seek a professional hypnotherapist.)

ACUPUNCTURE

The ancient Chinese tradition of acupuncture has long been used to cure all sorts of mental and physical ailments, from pain to depression. If you're feeling anxious, acupuncture sessions with a trained practitioner, in which fine needles are inserted in the skin along energy lines or "meridians", could help to release muscle tension and make you feel calmer.

EPSOM SALTS

While it's important to eat lots of
magnesium-rich foods, there are
other ways you can feel the powerful
benefits of this magic mineral. One
alternative therapy for anxiety is to
take a bath with Epsom salts dissolved
in it. The salts help your body
absorb magnesium through the skin,
making you feel more relaxed. Seek
out these magic salts in your local
health store or large supermarket.

I learned
that
courage
was not the
absence
of **fear**,
but the
triumph
over it.
The **brave**
man is not he
who does not feel
afraid, but he
who **conquers**
that fear.

NELSON MANDELA

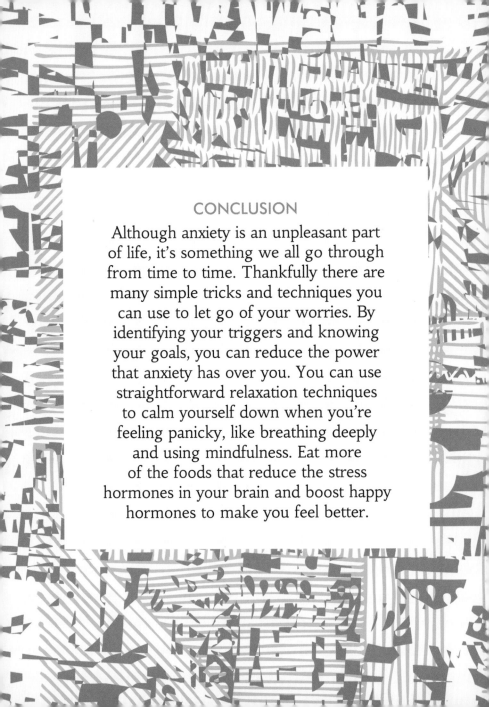

CONCLUSION

Although anxiety is an unpleasant part of life, it's something we all go through from time to time. Thankfully there are many simple tricks and techniques you can use to let go of your worries. By identifying your triggers and knowing your goals, you can reduce the power that anxiety has over you. You can use straightforward relaxation techniques to calm yourself down when you're feeling panicky, like breathing deeply and using mindfulness. Eat more of the foods that reduce the stress hormones in your brain and boost happy hormones to make you feel better.

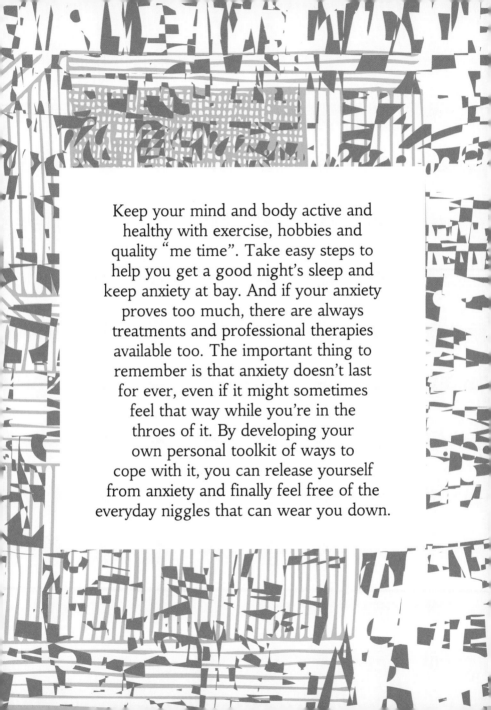

Keep your mind and body active and healthy with exercise, hobbies and quality "me time". Take easy steps to help you get a good night's sleep and keep anxiety at bay. And if your anxiety proves too much, there are always treatments and professional therapies available too. The important thing to remember is that anxiety doesn't last for ever, even if it might sometimes feel that way while you're in the throes of it. By developing your own personal toolkit of ways to cope with it, you can release yourself from anxiety and finally feel free of the everyday niggles that can wear you down.

No one outside
ourselves
can rule us
inwardly.
When we
know this, we
become free.

Buddha

FURTHER READING

These websites are great starting points for more information on anxiety and how to deal with it:

Anxiety UK
anxietyuk.org.uk

Mind
mind.org.uk

Alternative therapies
adaa.org/finding-help/treatment/complementary-alternative-treatment

Cognitive behavioural therapy
www.nhs.uk/conditions/cognitive-behavioural-therapy-cbt

If you're interested in finding out more
about our books, find us on Facebook at
Summersdale Publishers and follow
us on Twitter at **@Summersdale**.

WWW.SUMMERSDALE.COM

IMAGE CREDITS

p.2 © Jason Heglund Illustration & Design; p.3 © Olga Kovalenkoe/Shutterstock.com; pp.4–5, 159 © Olly Molly/Shutterstock.com; pp.6–7 © OKing/Shutterstock.com; pp.8, 9, 12, 18, 42, 43, 57 (background), 90, 91, 102, 138, 134, 139 © Lera Efremova/Shutterstock.com; p.10 © Nikolaeva/Shutterstock.com; pp.11, 26–27, 40, 61 © Softulka/Shutterstock.com; pp.13, 28 © ibom/Shutterstock.com; pp.14, 23, 32, 33, 44, 153 © miniwide/Shutterstock.com; pp.15, 21, 95, 112, 143 © cosmaa/Shutterstock.com; p.16 © Gluiki/Shutterstock.com; p.19 © Natalya Levish/Shutterstock.com; pp.20, 22 © Dean Drobot/Shutterstock.com; pp.24, 35, 121 © helterskelter/Shutterstock.com; p.25 © Mjosedesign/Shutterstock.com; pp.29, 30, 36, 39, 49, 57 (glasses), 79, 109 (phone), 114 (drawing) 145 © ValeriSerg/Shutterstock.com; p.37 © Kubko/Shutterstock.com; p.38 © Nenilkime/Shutterstock.com; p.41 © Ann Muse/Shutterstock.com; p.45 © Nikiparonak/Shutterstock.com; p.46 © aniok/Shutterstock.com; p.47 © Sundry Studio/Shutterstock.com; p.48 © Anastasiya Samolovova/Shutterstock.com; pp.50, 105 © geraria/Shutterstock.com; p.51 © wectors/Shutterstock.com; p.52 © Sasikumar3g/Shutterstock.com; p.53 © VectorShow/Shutterstock.com; p.54 © Monash/Shutterstock.com; p.55 © sibiranna/Shutterstock.com; p.58 © lena7391/Shutterstock.com; p.59 © anna42f/Shutterstock.com; p.60 © Meow Wanvilai/Shutterstock.com; p.62 © hchjjl/Shutterstock.com; p.63 © Madiwaso/Shutterstock.com; p.66 © My Life Graphic/Shutterstock.com; p.67 © Aleksei Derin/Shutterstock.com; p.68 © alinabel/Shutterstock.com; p.69 © Ohmega1982/Shutterstock.com; p.70 © hartgraphic/Shutterstock.com; p.71 © one line man/Shutterstock.com; p.72 © jesadaphorn/Shutterstock.com; p.73 © Auttapon Wongtakeaw/Shutterstock.com; p.74 © Nadia Grapes/Shutterstock.com; p.75 © Tasiania/Shutterstock.com; p.76 © shekaka/Shutterstock.com; pp.77, 140 © nikiteev_konstantin/Shutterstock.com; p.78 © tsaplia/Shutterstock.com; p.80 © Natasha_Chetkova/Shutterstock.com; p.81 © Irina Shatilova/Shutterstock.com; p.82 © Manekina Serafima/Shutterstock.com; p.83 © Dasha D/Shutterstock.com; p.84 © ArtMari/Shutterstock.com; p.85 © OlyaSenko/Shutterstock.com; p.86 © Natata/Shutterstock.com; p.87 © Vera Serg/Shutterstock.com; p.88 © pickbiz/Shutterstock.com; pp.89, 103 © Veronika By/Shutterstock.com; p.92 © PONYHEAD/Shutterstock.com; p.93 © inroad/Shutterstock.com; p.94 © v.ronnica/Shutterstock.com; p.97 © zubdash/Shutterstock.com; p.100 © art of line/Shutterstock.com; p.101 © kiyanochka1/Shutterstock.com; p.108 © Iraida Bearlala/Shutterstock.com; p.109 © Avector (hearts)/Shutterstock.com; pp.110, 111 © Cienpies Design/Shutterstock.com; p.114 © TairA (background)/Shutterstock.com; p.115 © Anna Kutukova/Shutterstock.com; p.116 © Freeda/Shutterstock.com; p.117 © Dragan Eric/Shutterstock.com; p.118 © venimo/Shutterstock.com; p.119 © tobrono/Shutterstock.com; p.122 © WindAwake/Shutterstock.com; p.123 © graphicES/Shutterstock.com; p.124 © Dzm1try/Shutterstock.com; p.126 © Larisa Glushkova/Shutterstock.com; p.127 © Loseva Marina/Shutterstock.com; p.128 © denk creative/Shutterstock.com; pp.129, 149, 150 © GoodStudio/Shutterstock.com; p.130 © mei yanotai/Shutterstock.com; p.131 © lineartestpilot/Shutterstock.com; p.132 © Victory1103/Shutterstock.com; p.133 © Franzi/Shutterstock.com; p.135 © Julia Korchevska/Shutterstock.com; p.136 © Croisy/Shutterstock.com; p.137 © iku4/Shutterstock.com; pp.141, 142 © Vanzyst/Shutterstock.com; p.144, 146, 147, 156–157 © jumpingsack/Shutterstock.com; p.148 © Saint A/Shutterstock.com; p.151 © Lano4ka/Shutterstock.com; p.152 © dobrodzei/Shutterstock.com; p.154 © Daniela Barreto/Shutterstock.com; p.155 © Snowboard School/Shutterstock.com; p.158 © Tanya Syrytsyna/Shutterstock.com